CW00687614

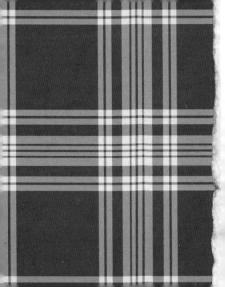

Clueless

LESSONS ON LOVE, FASHION, AND FRIENDSHIP

RP MINIS

PHILADELPHIA

RP Minis™
Hachette Book Group
1290 Avenue of the Americas, New York, NY 10104
www.runningpress.com
@Running_Press

Printed in China

First Edition: April 2020

Published by RP Minis, an imprint of Perseus Books, LLC, a subsidiary of Hachette Book Group, Inc. The RP Minis name and logo is a trademark of the Hachette Book Group.

The Hachette Speakers Bureau provides a wide range of authors for speaking events. To find out more, go to www.hachettespeakersbureau.com or call (866) 376-6591.

The publisher is not responsible for websites (or their content) that are not owned by the publisher.

Library of Congress Control Number: 2019952341

ISBN: 978-0-7624-7033-4 (hardcover),
978-0-7624-9708-9 (ebook)

LREX

10 9 8 7 6 5 4 3 2 1

Contents

The Kids in America

So, okay. Here's the 411 on the 1995 cinematic masterpiece *Clueless*. The coming-of-age teen comedy reimagines Jane Austen's *Emma* in the mansions and malls of Beverly Hills. The brain child of Amy Heckerling (who's like, a totally important filmmaker), *Clueless* follows popular girl Cher Horowitz and her girlfriends as they navigate high school hallways, the rules of the road, and Val parties gone wrong. Through the trials and tribulations of these well-to-do teens, Heckerling proves that there might be a thing or two to learn from the adorably clueless.

Take self-assured Cher, for example. Our leading lady is a

trend-setting, mansion-living, report card-arguing friend of Dionne who is waiting on a Baldwin. While Cher insists that her life is far from the fantasy world of a Noxzema ad, her flawless skin, well-coordinated confidantes, and virtual wardrobe make a different case about her reality. Oblivious to her own privilege, Cher is good-hearted and wants to use her popularity to help others live the good life too—whether by playing matchmaker for her teachers or making over the new girl Tai into a part of the popular crew. While she means well, it's through a few errors in judgment and misguided deeds that Cher soon realizes that *she* needed an inner makeover all along.

In the end, *Clueless* isn't really about the search for the perfect partner, plaid outfit, or popularity—well, it is and it isn't. It's about embracing who you are, learning from your mistakes, and always putting your best platform forward to help your friends, family, and most importantly—yourself!

This little book of advice, quick tips, and quotes from Cher and the Beverly Hills elite is here to inspire and empower as you navigate life in a post-1995 world. After all, teenagers

like Cher are just trying to get
through it like the rest of us,
one "as if" at a time.

Do what you love!

Dionne:
Cher's main thrill in life is a makeover, okay? It gives her a sense of control in a world full of chaos.

Teach your children well.

Mel: You mean to tell me that you argued your way from a "C+" to an "A-"?

Cher: Totally based on my powers of persuasion. Are you proud?

Mel: Honey, I couldn't be happier than if they were based on real grades.

Deep Thoughts with Travis

Tardiness is not something you can do all on your own. Many, many people contribute to my tardiness. Uh, I'd like to thank my parents for never giving me a ride to school. The L.A. City bus drivers for taking a chance on an unknown kid. And last, but not least, the wonderful crew at McDonald's for

Give credit where it's due.

Dionne: Phat! Did you write that?

Cher: Duh! It's like a famous quote.

Dionne: From where?

Cher: Cliff's Notes.

All things in
moderation.

Understand context.

Mel: You drink?

Christian: No, thanks. I'm cool.

Mel: I'm not offering. I'm asking you if you drink. You think I'd give alcohol to teenage drivers taking my daughter out?

22

Follow doctors' orders.

Amber: Miss Stoeger, my plastic surgeon doesn't want me doing any activity where balls fly at my nose.

Dionne: Well, there goes your social life.

Things are not always what they seem.

Cher: Oh, she's a full-on Monet.

Tai: What's a Monet?

Cher: It's like the paintings, see? From far away it's okay, but up close it's a big ole mess.

Take time to recharge.

Cher: I felt impotent and out of control, which I really hate. I needed to find sanctuary in a place where I could gather my thoughts and regain my strength.

You can't talk your way out of everything.

Driving instructor: Well, let's see, shall we? You can't park. You can't switch lanes. You can't make right-hand turns. You've damaged private property and you almost killed someone. Offhand, I'd say you failed.

Rollin' with
the Homies

Find your people— through whatever connection.

Cher: Dionne and I were both named after great singers of the past who now do infomercials.

Honesty is the best policy.

Cher: Would you call me selfish?

Dionne: No, not to your face.

Be supportive.

Tai: Cher, you're a virgin?

Sulk
together.

Cher: Let's blow off
seventh and eighth,
go to the mall, have a
calorie fest, and see the
new Christian Slater.

Lift your friends up.

Lawrence: It's the bomb!

Murray: You know what I'm sayin'? You look good!

Lawrence: As will you.

Empower them.

Christian: The jacket . . . is it James Dean or Jason Priestly?

Cher: Carpe diem, okay? You looked hot in it.

Words hurt.

Tai: You're a virgin who can't drive.

47

Hug it out.

Tai: Oh, Cher, I'm really sorry. Oh shit . . . now I'm gonna go ahead and cry.

Butt-Crazy in Love

Love is patient.

Cher: Searching for a boy in high school is as useless as searching for meaning in a Pauly Shore movie.

Love is kind.

Cher: Old people can be so sweet.

It does
not envy.

Murray: Where you been all weekend? What's up? You jeepin' behind my back?

It does not boast.

Elton: Don't you even know who my father is?

Cher: Oh . . . you are a snob and a half.

There's nothing wrong with being selective.

Cher: I mean, you saw how picky I am about my shoes and they only go on my feet.

Deep Thoughts with Tai

If I'm too good for him, then how come I'm not with him?

Cher: Ugh! As if!

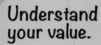

Understand your value.

Cher: During the next few days I did what any normal girl would do, I sent myself love letters and flowers and candy just so he'd see how desired I was, in case he didn't already know.

Leave them wanting more.

Cher: Make sure Elton sees you, but don't say "hi" first. Pretend like you're having fun and you're really popular. Talk to someone in his eye line, preferably a guy. Make him come to you. And find an excuse to leave while he's still into the conversation.

Treat your partner with respect.

Dionne: Murray, I've asked you repeatedly not to call me "woman"!

Murray: Excuse me, Miss Dionne.

It's all about give and take.

Cher: I suppose it wasn't meant to be. I mean, he does dress better than I do. What would I bring to the relationship?

With self-love, comes real love.

Fashion
Forward

Be bold.

Cher: Go shopping with Dr. Seuss?

Dionne: Well, at least I wouldn't skin a collie to make my backpack.

Cher: It's faux.

Confidence is everything.

Mel: What the hell is that?

Cher: A dress.

Mel: Says who?

Cher: Calvin Klein.

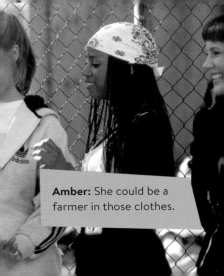

Amber: She could be a farmer in those clothes.

Break out of your comfort zone.

Cher: Did you notice any positive changes in her?

Josh: Yeah, under your tutelage she's exploring the challenging world of bare midriffs.

Deep Thoughts with Cher

So, okay, I don't want to be a traitor to my generation and all, but I don't get how guys dress today. I mean, come on, it looks, like they just fell out of bed and put on some baggy pants and take their greasy hair, eww!, and cover it up with a backwards cap, and like, we're expected to swoon? I don't think so.

Be a leader, not a follower.

Dionne: When I get married I'm gonna have a sailor dress, but it's gonna be a gown. And then all my bridesmaids are gonna wear sailor hats with veils.

Know when to ask for help.

Cher: Do you prefer "fashion victim" or "ensemble-y challenged"?

Dress for the job you want.

Cher: Lucy! Where's my white collarless shirt from Fred Segal? It's my most capable-looking outfit.

A picture is worth a thousand words.

Cher: I don't rely on mirrors, so I always take Polaroids.

Fashion is suffering.

Josh: Hey, James Bond, in America we drive on the right side of the road.

Cher: I am! You try driving in platforms.

No designer dress is worth dying over.

Cher: Oh, no. You don't understand. This is an Alaïa!

Robber: An A-what-uh?

Cher: It's like a totally important designer.

Robber: And I will totally shoot you in the head.

kend Homework

FUN!

Giving Back

Help the less fortunate.

Cher: It's like that book I read in ninth grade that said, "'Tis a far, far better thing doing stuff for other people."

Put your skills to good use.

Cher: Oh, sure, she has runs in her stockings and her slip is always showing and she has more lipstick on her teeth than on her mouth. God, this woman is screaming for a makeover. I'm her only hope.

It's dope to be kind.

Cher: Hey, you know what would be so dope? If we got some really delicious take-out. I bet they haven't eaten all night.

Josh: Yeah, that would be pretty dope of us.

Think globally,
act locally.

Josh: Hey, y'know, in some parts
of the universe, maybe not in
Contempo Casual, but in some
parts, it's considered cool to
know what's going on in this
world.

It's never too late to start.

Josh: You're so quiet. Haven't made me watch *The Real World*.

Cher: I care about the news.

Josh: Since when?

Cher: Since now.

Deep Thoughts with Cher

Like right now, for example, the Haitians need to come to America. But some people are all, "What about the strain on our resources?" But it's like, when I had this garden party for my father's birthday, right?

I said RSVP because it was a sit-down dinner. But people came that like did not RSVP. So, I was like totally buggin'. And so if the government could just get to the kitchen, rearrange some things, we could certainly party with the Haitians. And in conclusion may I please remind you . . .

Tolerance is always a good lesson.

Travis: Like, the way I feel about the Rolling Stones is the way my kids are gonna feel about Nine Inch Nails, so I really shouldn't torment my mom anymore, huh?

It's better to give than to receive.

Mel: I don't think they need your skis.

Cher: Daddy, some people lost all their belongings, don't you think that includes athletic equipment?

Be the change you wish to see in the world.

Cher: Excuse me, but I have donated many expensive Italian outfits to Lucy and, as soon as I get my license, I fully intend to brake for animals. And I've contributed many hours helping two lonely teachers find romance.

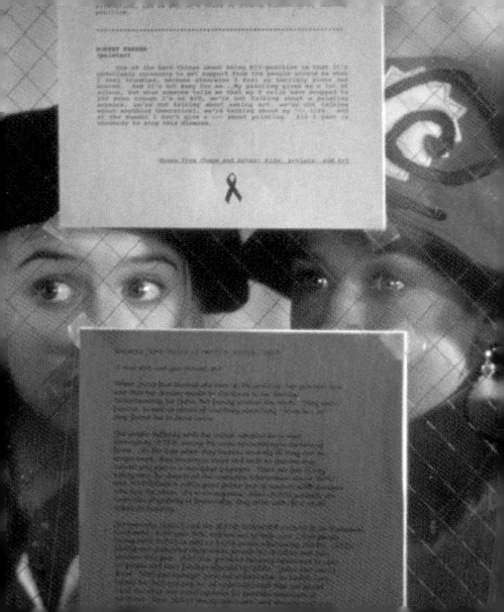

To Thine Own
Self be True

Practice what you preach.

Cher: I decided I needed a complete makeover. But this time . . . I'd make over my soul.

Nobody's perfect.

Cher: Everything I think and everything I do is wrong.

Sometimes you
"can't even,"
and that's okay.

Amber: Whatever.

Deep Thoughts with Murray

Okay, but street slang is an increasingly valid form of expression. Most of the feminine pronouns do have mocking, but not necessarily misogynistic, undertone.

Expand your vocabulary.

Josh: Be seein' ya.

Tai: Yeah, I hope not sporadically.

Read for pleasure.

Cher: My first book is *Fit or Fat.*

Tai: Mine is *Men are from Mars, Women are from Venus.*

There's no shame in the human body.

Cher: Mr. Hall, I was surfing the crimson wave. I had to haul ass to the ladies.

Keep doing you.

Dionne: Why did you do this to your head?

Murray: 'Cause I'm keeping it real. 'Cause I'm keeping it real.

This book has been bound using handcraft methods and Smyth-sewn to ensure durability.

Quotes from the *Clueless* screenplay written by Amy Heckerling.

Additional text by Lauren Mancuso.

Designed by Nnyji Whitfield.

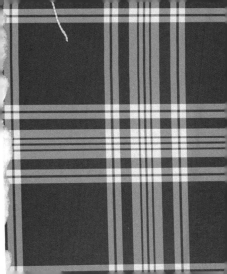